Linking art to the world around us

artyfact

Space

Abbey
Children's

CONCEPT

Publisher: Felicia Law

Design: Tracy Carrington

Editorial Planning: Karen Foster

Research and Development: Gerry Bailey, Alec Edgington

PROJECT DEVELOPMENT

Project Director: Karen Foster

Editors: Claire Sipi, Hazel Songhurst, Samantha Sweeney

Design Director: Tracy Carrington

Design Manager: Flora Awolaja

Design and DTP: Claire Penny, Paul Montague,
James Thompson, Mark Dempsey

Photo and Art Editor: Andrea Sadler

Illustrator: Jan Smith

Model Artist: Sophie Dean

Further models: Sue Partington, Abigail Dean

Digital Workflow: Edward MacDermott

Production: Victoria Grimsell, Christina Brown

Scanning: Acumen Colour Ltd

Published by Abbey Children's Books
(a division of Abbey Home Media Group)

Abbey Home Media Group
435-437 Edgware Road
London W2 1TH
United Kingdom

Printed and bound by Dai Nippon, Hong Kong

FRONT COVER IMAGES: MAX-PLANCK-INSTITUT FUR EXTRATERRESTRISCHE PHYSIK/ SCIENCE PHOTO LIBRARY; ASTROFOTO/ BRUCE COLEMAN COLLECTION; NASA

Linking art to the world around us

artyfacts
Space

Contents

WRITTEN BY Polly Goodman

Solar system

Earth is one of the nine planets in our solar system. The Sun is at the centre of the solar system, and the planets orbit on a circular path around it. The solar system was formed over 4 billion years ago from a swirling mass of gas, dust and ice. As the Sun was forming, some of the matter was pulled together into clumps by the force of gravity.

BIG AND SMALL CLUMPS
The newly formed clumps close to the Sun were mostly made of heavy, rock-like matter. The Sun's powerful heat pushed away the lighter, more gaseous matter and it collected together in masses further away.

JOINED-UP CLUMPS
In time, the clumps joined together, to form the nine planets we know. Smaller chunks of matter that did not form into either planets or moons orbiting the planets, sometimes crashed into them. Our own moon is covered with craters formed from these impacts.

NINE PLANETS AND ASTEROID BELT
The inner planets have been named Mercury, Venus, Earth and Mars. The outer planets are called Jupiter, Saturn, Uranus, Neptune and Pluto. There may be other planets further out in the solar system. Between Mars and Jupiter lies the 'asteroid belt', made up of thousands of small, odd-shaped clumps of rock that slowly orbit the Sun. The asteroid belt was probably made up of clumps that did not form into full-sized planets when the solar system was born.

Space

Add spiral galaxies and sparkling discs

WHAT YOU NEED

newspaper

bucket

paste

glue

paints and brush

needle

wire

bamboo sticks

1 Tear off pieces of newspaper and soak them overnight in a bucket of water.

2 Squeeze as much as you can of the water from the soaked paper.

3 Make planets by dipping the paper into the paste and moulding it into several different size balls. Leave these to dry.

4 Paint your planets different colours.

5 Push the darning needle through the middle of each ball and thread a length of wire, fixing it with glue.

6 Make wire stars and different galaxy shapes to add to your mobile.

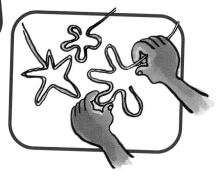

Tie two bamboo sticks together in a cross. Hang your stars, planets and galaxies from them.

Blue world

WATER, LAND AND AIR

As far as we know, Earth is the only planet in the solar system where there is life. It is the only planet with liquid water on its surface and oxygen in its atmosphere. The Earth's landscapes vary from rocky mountaintops to green valleys; from dry, barren deserts to hot, wet rainforests. At the Antarctic, the land is almost completely covered in ice. Surrounding the Earth is its atmosphere – a layer of gases – which protects the Earth from the Sun's harmful rays, and keeps it warm like a blanket.

SPINNING GLOBE

The Earth spins like a top as it travels around the Sun. It spins around its axis, an imaginary line that runs through the middle of Earth from north to south. Its spinning motion causes day and night, as each side of the Earth faces towards and then away from the Sun. It takes 365 days – a year – for Earth to travel around the Sun. Since the Earth's axis is tilted, its movement around the Sun causes seasons to change. The northern part of Earth tilts towards the Sun in summer and away from the Sun in winter.

If you were an astronaut floating in space, planet Earth would look like a huge blue ball with swirling white patterns on its surface. Its blue colour comes from the vast oceans that cover Earth's surface. The swirling white patterns are clouds. You would also see the black emptiness of outer space all around the planet.

EARTH'S MAGNETIC FIELD

We live on a huge magnet! All around the Earth is a giant magnetic field, just like the magnetic field around a bar magnet. What makes the Earth magnetic? Deep inside the Earth, there's a core of hot molten metal. Because our world is always spinning, this causes electric currents in the molten metal. These currents create the magnetic field around the Earth.

Space

Fridge magnets

Fridge magnets

WHAT YOU NEED

clay

magnets

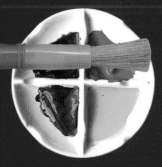

paints and brush

glue

Decorate your fridge with shiny magnetic space shapes

1 Soften the clay and mould into a set of space shapes as shown.

2 When dry, paint.

3 Glue magnets to the backs of the space shapes.

7

Spectacular Sun

The Sun is a giant ball of burning gases, hotter than we could ever imagine. It is a star, like the billions of other stars in the Universe, but it seems bigger than other stars because it is closer to Earth. The Sun is the most important star to Earth because it provides heat and light that are essential for life on our planet.

LIGHT AND HEAT ENERGY

Deep in the core, or centre, of the Sun, the temperature is 15 million°C! At this temperature, the particles of gas that make up the Sun react together to make nuclear energy. The energy travels out from the centre and eventually escapes from the surface as light and heat.

SURFACE AND ATMOSPHERE

The Sun's surface is called the photosphere. It is here that the light and heat energy is given off. Surrounding the photosphere are millions of kilometres of the Sun's atmosphere. It is made up of two main parts: the chromosphere, a hotter inner layer, and the corona, which is the outermost layer of the atmosphere. Throughout the atmosphere, explosions of gases, called flares, erupt. Gigantic arches of gases, called prominences, stretch from the chromosphere to the corona.

SUNSPOTS

The surface of the Sun is speckled with dark-looking areas, called sunspots. These spots occur where the Sun's magnetism on the surface is so strong that it cools down certain areas, making them appear darker.

SOLAR WINDS

As the Sun's hot gases expand from the corona, they form solar winds that spiral outwards into space. The winds extend 15 billion kilometres from the Sun, reaching speeds of between 250 to 1,000 kilometres a second. As they travel past the Earth, the solar winds squeeze its magnetic field into a teardrop shape.

Sun-catcher

WHAT YOU NEED

wire

tissue paper

scissors

glitter

gold paper

glue

clear and coloured acetate

gold string

beads

1 Make a circle from wire. Create solar flares by twisting the wire into flame shapes as you go round again.

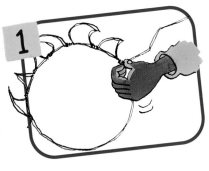

2 Tear and cut pieces of tissue paper, acetate and gold paper and patch over the wire circle to cover.

3 Glue on glittery sunspots and attach a piece of gold string threaded with beads to the top – and hang.

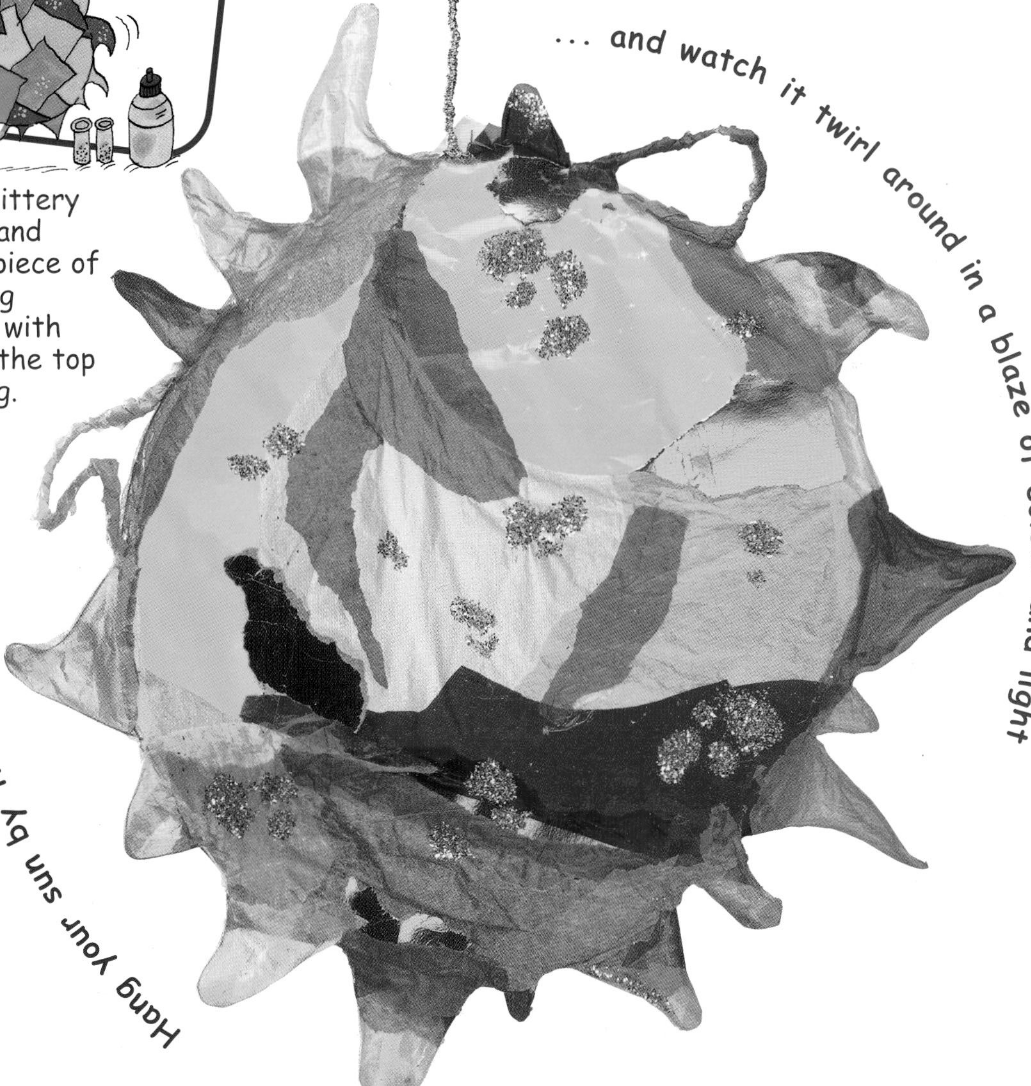

... and watch it twirl around in a blaze of colour and light

Hang your sun by the window ...

9

Mysterious Moon

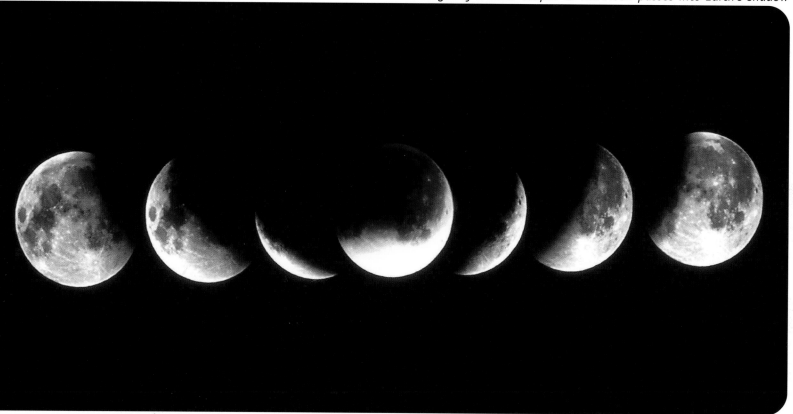

The Moon is the Earth's closest neighbour. It is a mysterious, lifeless companion, captured by the Earth's gravity into constantly circling our planet. It is the only other world that humans have visited.

NEW MOON TO NEW MOON

The Moon has no light of its own. It shines because it reflects light from the Sun. As it travels around the Earth, we see different parts of the Moon lit up. It takes about a month for the Moon to circle the Earth, so the Moon follows a cycle that is repeated every month. The cycle starts with a new Moon, when the Moon looks completely dark. This is because it is between the Sun and the Earth, so the side facing us is in darkness. Over the next two weeks, the sunlit part of the Moon gets bigger. It becomes a crescent, a half Moon and a full Moon. Then the pattern reverses and the sunlit part gets smaller, from full Moon to half Moon and then new Moon again.

LUNAR ECLIPSE

Once or twice a year, when the Moon should be full, it passes through the Earth's shadow. This means the Moon's face gets darker, causing a lunar eclipse. In a total lunar eclipse, the whole Moon passes through the central, darkest part of the Earth's shadow. In a partial eclipse, part of the Moon is in the central part of the shadow and the rest is in the paler edge.

Space

Make black and white crescent moon pictures for your bedroom wall

WHAT YOU NEED

black and white paint

paintbrush

black and white paper

glitter

pencil

glue

mounting card

1 Draw the outline of a crescent moon in different sizes and thicknesses.

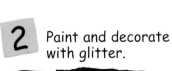

2 Paint and decorate with glitter.

3 Mount on card.

11

Mighty Jupiter

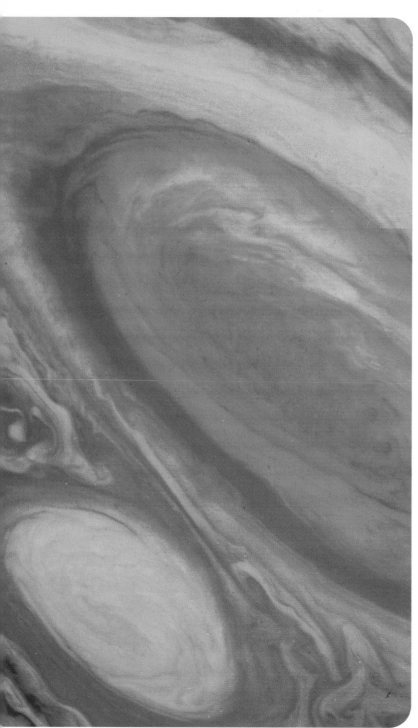

Jupiter is the biggest and heaviest planet in the solar system. Through binoculars you can see its four largest moons as they circle the planet. If you looked through a telescope, you would see multi-coloured bands of clouds surrounding this giant ball of gas – and its faint ring of dust.

STORMY PLANET

A day on Jupiter lasts just 9 hours and 55 minutes compared to Earth's 24 hours, since this is the time it takes for Jupiter to spin on its axis. Its spinning speed whips up whirling winds of over 600 kilometres an hour. Storms on this mighty planet can even be seen from Earth. Jupiter's storms blow its clouds into ever-changing patterns.

GREAT RED SPOT

For over 300 years, a hurricane called the Great Red Spot has been spiralling in Jupiter's atmosphere. The hurricane is three times the size of Earth. It hovers 8 kilometres above the clouds, drawing up damp air and whipping it into a spiral. When the hurricane is very strong, it shows up as a deep red spot against the rest of the planet's creamy colour. When it is weaker, the hurricane can be difficult to see.

JUPITER'S MOONS

Jupiter has at least 16 moons. They range in size from Ganymede, which is 5,268 kilometres wide, to the tiny Leda, with a diameter of only 10 kilometres.

A close-up view of Jupiter's Great Red Spot

Space

WHAT YOU NEED

- balloon
- newspaper
- glue
- paint and brush
- foil cake cup
- gold thread
- glass beads
- beads
- scissors
- sequins

1

Blow up the balloon. Rip pieces of newspaper and glue all over the balloon, building up several layers. Leave to dry.

Paint and splatter on yellow, orange and red colours for a stripey, marbled effect.

2

3

Flatten the foil cake cup and glue glass beads and sequins onto it.

4

Pop and discard the balloon. Decorate a length of gold thread with threaded, glued on beads and sequins and attach to the top of your model.

Hang your stripey Jupiter mobile from the ceiling and admire its jewelled 'red spot'.

Glue the decorated foil cake cup into place.

Starry patterns

O n a clear night, the sky twinkles with thousands of stars. One way to start finding your way around the night sky is by looking for a familiar, bright star and then locating other stars from it. Up to 2,500 stars are visible with the naked eye. With binoculars and telescopes, you might be able to see up to 6,000.

CONSTELLATIONS

Constellations are patterns made by the stars. Star maps show the shapes of constellations by joining the stars in each with lines, like a dot-to-dot puzzle. The ancient Arabs, Greeks and Romans named many constellations after animals or figures they saw in the patterns. The Pleiades were named after seven sisters in an ancient Greek myth.

BRIGHTEST STAR

In the northern hemisphere, one of the easiest constellations to find is the Plough. It is visible all year round. Look for a saucepan shape made up of seven stars. The edge of the saucepan points towards the North Star, or Pole star, which is in almost exactly the same position every night, above the North Pole. The brightest star in the northern hemisphere is Arcturus, which is part of a constellation called the Herdsman. The brightest star of all is Sirius, or the Dog Star. Sirius can only be seen from the southern hemisphere. It is part of a constellation called Canis Major. In the southern hemisphere, the Southern Cross is the most well known feature of the night sky.

The Pleiades constellation

Space

Constellations

Create a night sky and fill it with amazing starry patterns

WHAT YOU NEED

- black card
- scissors
- toothbrush
- glitter
- gold thread
- metallic paints
- paintbrush
- glue
- white card
- glitter glue
- shiny paper

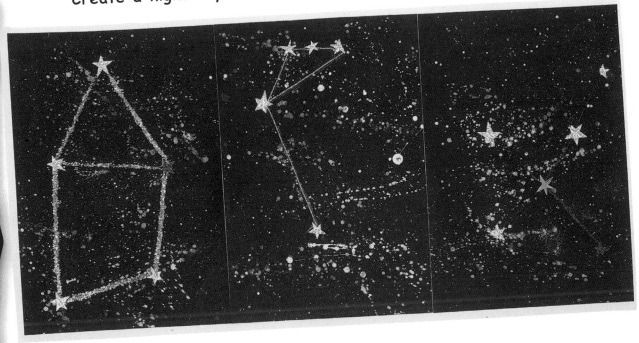

1 Use your paint and brush to splatter patterns on pieces of black card.

2 Cut stars from the shiny paper and glue to the black card in fantasy constellation shapes.

3 Join the shiny stars together with glitter glue, or by sticking on gold thread.

4 Mount onto white card.

15

The red planet

Mars is one of Earth's closest neighbours. It is red because of the iron in its soil and rocks. When winds blow up red dust from the ground, they create strawberry-coloured skies. Mars was named after the Roman god of war, because red is the colour of blood, anger and warfare.

LIFE ON MARS

For over 300 years, people have been wondering whether there is life on Mars. Its surface is more like Earth's than any other planet and it has clouds, weather and an atmosphere. But in 1965, when the space probe Mariner 4 sent back the first photographs of Mars' surface, hopes of life on the planet were dashed. The photographs showed a desolate-looking landscape, with no surface water. However, scientists believe that Mars used to have surface water in the past, and that it may now be frozen under ice. In 1996, a meteorite that fell on to Antarctica from Mars thousands of years ago was discovered. The meteorite contained fossils of bacteria and other evidence of living organisms on Mars. It is possible that there was once life on Mars a very long time ago. However, many scientists believe it is unlikely that life still exists on the planet.

MARS VISITOR

On 4 July 1997, the Pathfinder spacecraft landed on Mars. It used a six-wheeled vehicle called the Sojourner Rover to explore the surroundings and test the soil and atmosphere using special instruments. Scientists on Earth used radio-control to direct Sojourner.

Space

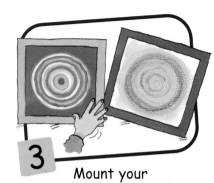

card

paints and brush

pastels

glue

coloured card

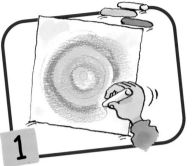

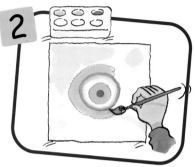

1 Draw pastel circles of different thicknesses on card. Overlap the colours as you go.

2 Repeat step one, this time with coloured paints.

3 Mount your circles on card.

Can you draw smooth, round circles?

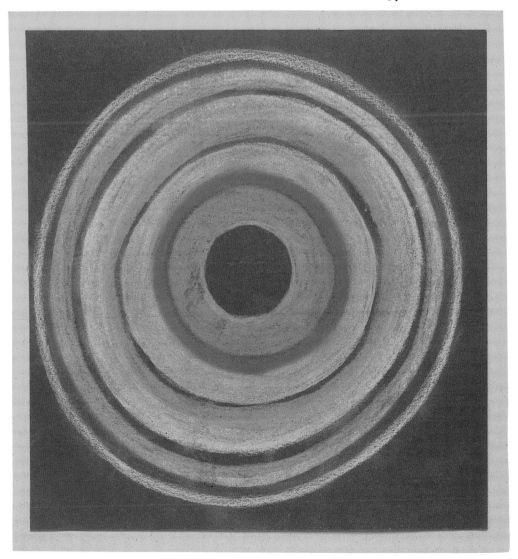

Dustclouds

Some of the most spectacular photographs taken in space show swirling clouds of glowing dust and gases. To the naked eye, these clouds are too faint to see.

Even with a telescope they are only small, pale smoke rings and smudges, although special cameras are able to pick up their colours and shapes.

WHAT ARE NEBULAE?

Nebulae are clouds of dust and gases. Their name comes from the Latin word for clouds. Most scientists believe that our whole solar system was formed from one giant, spiralling nebula. There are two main types of nebulae: planetary nebulae and diffuse nebulae.

PLANETARY NEBULAE

When a star dies, it throws off its outer layers, which form into glowing clouds of gas and dust. These clouds are called planetary nebulae.

HOT AND COLD STARS

Diffuse nebulae are even bigger than planetary nebulae. Astronomers have divided diffuse nebulae into three different types: emission, reflection and dark nebulae. Emission, or glowing, nebulae form near an extremely hot star. The star gives off so much ultraviolet light that gases in the cloud are heated up and glow. Reflection nebulae form when a cloud is near a cool star. The star is not hot enough to heat the gases in the cloud, but its light is reflected off dust in the cloud. These nebulae are bluish in colour. Dark nebulae are dark smudges against brighter clouds. They form where there are no stars nearby to reflect their light or the cloud blocks out light from stars behind it.

Different gases in this nebula glow in amazing colours.

Smudge art

Space

WHAT YOU NEED

- black paper
- mounting card
- glue
- sequins
- silver and white paint
- toothbrush
- pastels

1 Dip the toothbrush in white and silver paint and make spots on the paper.

Paint two dramatic night skies lit up by glowing stars and bright, pastel dustclouds

2 Use pastels and smudge the colours so they blend together.

3 Glue on an occasional sequin.

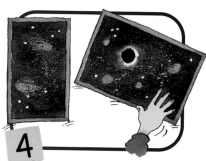

4 Mount your pictures.

Floating in space

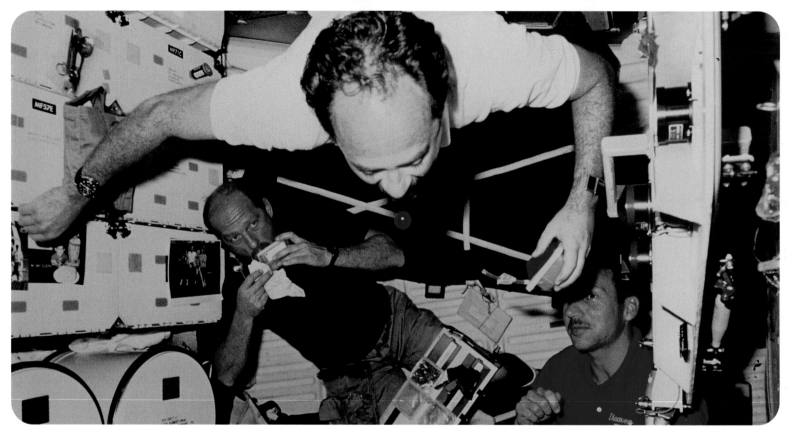

Imagine eating a biscuit and the crumbs floating away in the air! That's just one of the bizarre things that astronauts have to live with in space, where there is no oxygen, water or gravity. Breathing, eating, drinking and sleeping are very different experiences on a space station.

GETTING AROUND

The biggest problem astronauts have to overcome is the lack of gravity in a space station. Everything has to be fixed down. When they walk around, the astronauts use footholds, handholds and special straps attached to walkways.

SPACE FOOD

Astronauts eat ready meals that are heated from frozen. Chunks of food are covered with a kind of jelly called gelatin to stop them floating away. Drinks do not stay in the cup so astronauts have to drink with a straw from plastic packs.

BREATHING AND SLEEPING

Since there is no air in space, filters and fans supply the station with oxygen and remove carbon dioxide breathed out by the crew. Astronauts wear seat belts attached to their beds to stop them floating around the space station when they are asleep. Space station toilets use air currents to suck waste away from astronauts' bodies and out through waste pipes.

Space

WHAT YOU NEED

small boxes and pots

ardboard tubes

plastic bottles

aint and brush

gold read

newspaper

equins

wire

foil

strong glue

paste

old paper

Hang your model by a thread and watch it revolve

1

Glue together the bottles, boxes, tubes and pots to create a weird and wonderful space station.

2

Paste on strips of newspaper, to cover.

3

When dry, paint and decorate with foil and sequins.

Glue wire to the probe, satellite and astronaut and connect them to the space station. They will bounce up and down on their wires, as though in space!

4

Create a probe, astronaut and satellite from little boxes. Decorate with foil, gold paper and sequin details.

Saturn's rings

Saturn is one of the most beautiful planets in the solar system. From Earth, to the naked eye, it looks simply like a yellow star, but through a telescope you can see a spectacular set of rings circling its equator. Beneath the rings is Saturn's atmosphere – layers of orange and yellow clouds covered with a creamy-coloured haze.

SATURN'S SPIN

Saturn is the sixth planet from the Sun, almost ten times farther from the Sun than Earth. It takes almost 30 years for Saturn to travel round the Sun, compared to the Earth's single year. But a day on Saturn is much shorter than a day on Earth. It takes just 10 hours and 39 minutes for Saturn to complete a spin compared to Earth's 24 hours.

LIQUID PLANET

Saturn is the second largest planet in the solar system. It is a giant ball of gas and liquid, covered with colourful bands of clouds.

RINGS AND RINGLETS

Saturn has seven main rings, but each one is made up of thousands of closely packed ringlets. The ringlets are made from billions of glittering icy fragments, ranging in size from giant icebergs to tiny particles of ice. Scientists think that long ago, comets caught by Saturn's gravity collided and broke into pieces, forming the rings. The rings are so thin and flat that whenever they are in line with Earth, they are invisible.

A close-up view of Saturn's spectacular rings

Space

Spangled bangles

WHAT YOU NEED

scissors

sequins

beads

glue

wire

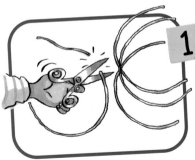

1 Make 4 to 5 semi-circles from the wire.

2 Thread and glue a variety of beads and sequins on to each.

Fasten your beaded bracelet around your wrist

3 Twist a piece of wire around the ends of the beaded strands so they are all fixed together.

4 Make a wire loop at one end and a hook at the other end, as shown.

23

A star is born

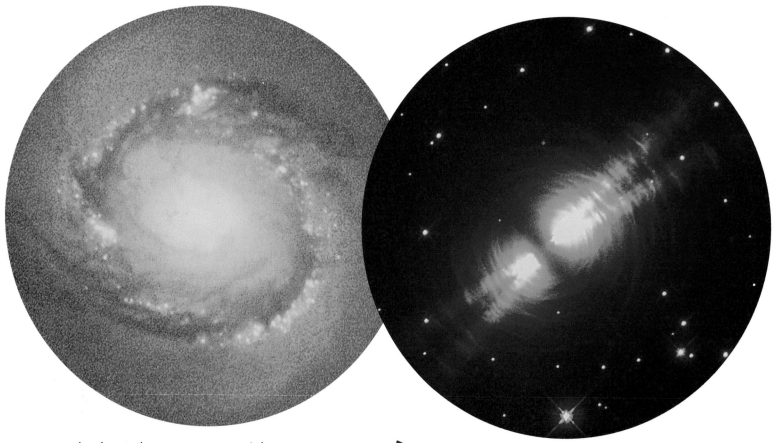

On a dark night, it is possible to see up to 2,500 different stars in the sky. The Sun is our nearest star, so it looks like a huge glowing ball. Other stars are much bigger than the Sun, but they are so far away that they look like pinpoints of light.

STAR BIRTH

A new star begins its life as a cloud of hydrogen, helium and dust. Over millions of years, gravity pulls these gases together into a ball. Nuclear energy is produced in the centre of the ball, heating the cloud around and making it glow. A new star is born.

DYING STARS

The bigger a star, the quicker it burns up its hydrogen and the shorter its life. As the hydrogen starts to run out, a star gets much bigger. Stars that have about the same mass as the Sun, or less than the Sun, gradually shed their outer layers. Only the core of the star remains. This is known as a 'white dwarf'. It gradually cools, becoming dimmer and redder, until it fades away completely. Stars of about five times the Sun's mass, and bigger, expand and become 'giants' or 'supergiants'. Some supergiants are a thousand times bigger than the Sun. Giants and supergiants eventually blow up in a massive explosion called a 'supernova', leaving behind either a 'neutron star' or a 'black hole'.

Stargazer

WHAT YOU NEED

card

glue

black and white paper

scissors

paper fastener

brush

glitter

silver paint

pastels

ruler

pencil

sequins

1 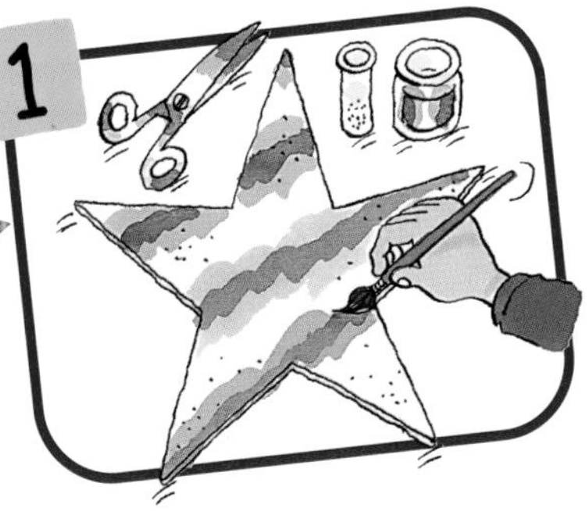 Draw and cut out a giant star. paint it silver and decorate it with sequins and glitter.

2 Draw and cut out two circles, one white, one black.

3 Divide the black circle into six equal segments. In each segment, use pastels to draw step-by-step pictures of the life of a star. Now glue circle to star.

4 Paint and decorate the white circle to match the silver star. Cut out a window big enough to show one of your pastel pictures.

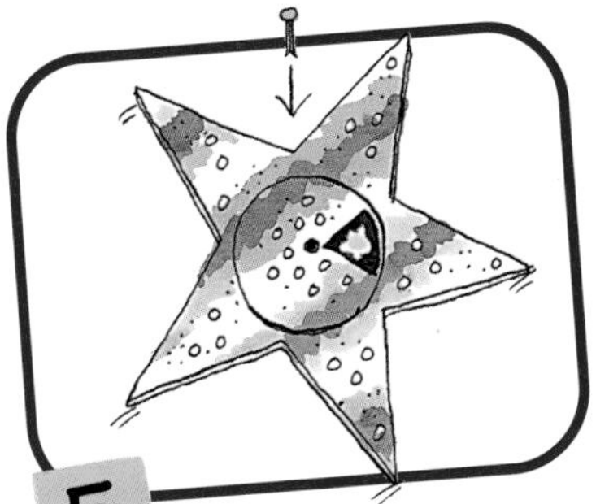

5 Attach the silver circle to the black one, using a paper fastener.

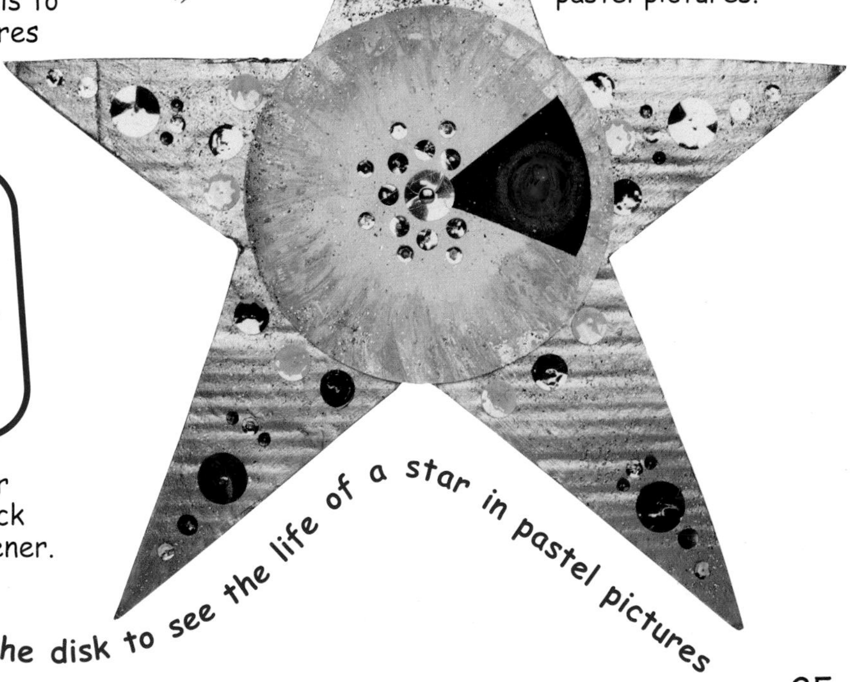

Turn the disk to see the life of a star in pastel pictures

25

Galactic swirls

The Universe is filled with many different kinds of galaxies. A galaxy is a system of stars, gas and dust held together by gravity. Astronomers do not know how many galaxies there are, but there are two main types, spiral galaxies and elliptical galaxies, so called because of their swirly shape and appearance.

Active galaxies

Some galaxies have most activity going on in their centres. These are called 'active galaxies'. Some active galaxies produce unusually strong radio waves. These are known as 'radio galaxies'. Quasars are another kind of active galaxy. They are the most distant objects astronomers know about. They look like stars, but are about 10,000 times brighter than a normal galaxy.

Jets of gas

The nearest radio galaxy to Earth is Centaurus A. It can be seen through binoculars as a tiny blob in the sky. A radio telescope shows it has huge jets of gas, called 'lobes', at either end of it. The jets give off light, radio waves and X-rays.

Black holes

When a massive star collapses at the end of its life, a black hole forms. Astronomers believe that at the centre of an active galaxy there is a giant black hole. As stars and other space debris fall towards the black hole, they form a hot swirling disc around the hole. The heat causes gas to flow off the disc in jets.

Space

Observatory

WHAT YOU NEED

paints and brush

plastic bottle

glue

box lid

scissors

newspaper

acetate

card

wire mesh

paste

1 Cut the bottom from a plastic bottle and paste on layers of newspaper.

2 Cut a triangular opening in the up-ended bottle. Now paint and decorate your observatory.

3 Cut one end off a box lid and cut diagonally along the sides to form a piece of card that will stand up. Paint a night sky scene on it. Glue fabric on a piece of card and paint a ground scene on this.

4 Use a rolled-up length of card to form the telescope. Fix and glue a piece of acetate over one end. Now wedge it inside the opening in the observatory.

5 Glue the observatory to the ground card. Slide the sky background behind it. Attach a triangular piece of wire mesh to half cover the telescope opening.

Use glowpaint to decorate your observatory for a night-time shimmer

Poison planet

V enus is one of the planets in our solar system and one of five planets we can actually see without a telescope. At certain times of the year, it is the first star to appear in the evening sky. Venus is about the same size as the Earth. Its year, the time it takes to orbit the Sun, is 225 Earth days. It is the only planet that rotates in the opposite direction to its orbit.

VENUS IN ORBIT

After Mercury, Venus is the second closest planet to the Sun. Its average distance from the Sun is about 108 million kilometres. Venus sometimes passes within 42 million kilometres of Earth – closer than any other planet.

ACID ATMOSPHERE

Venus is covered by thick clouds of sulphur and sulphuric acid. Space probes from Earth have explored the planet's surface. This is hot and dry, with mountains, canyons, valleys and flat plains. Two of the mountain ranges are bigger than any on Earth. Some areas are covered by a fine layer of dust; other areas are littered with sharp-edged rocks, and there may be some active volcanoes.

WATERLESS WORLD

There is no moisture on the surface of Venus. This is so hot that any water would immediately boil away. The atmosphere is mostly made up of carbon dioxide, with nitrogen gases and some water vapour. The pressure of the atmosphere, caused by the weight of these gases, is about 90 times heavier than on Earth. This heavy 'air' on Venus would squash a human. Life as we know it could not exist there because of the fierce heat and lack of enough oxygen.

PASSING SPACECRAFT

On 15 December 1970, the Soviet spacecraft Venera 7 landed on Venus. Since then, a number of further landings have sent back photographs of its atmosphere and surface.

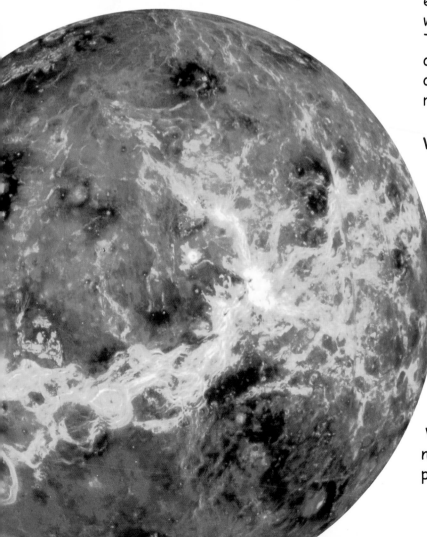

Space

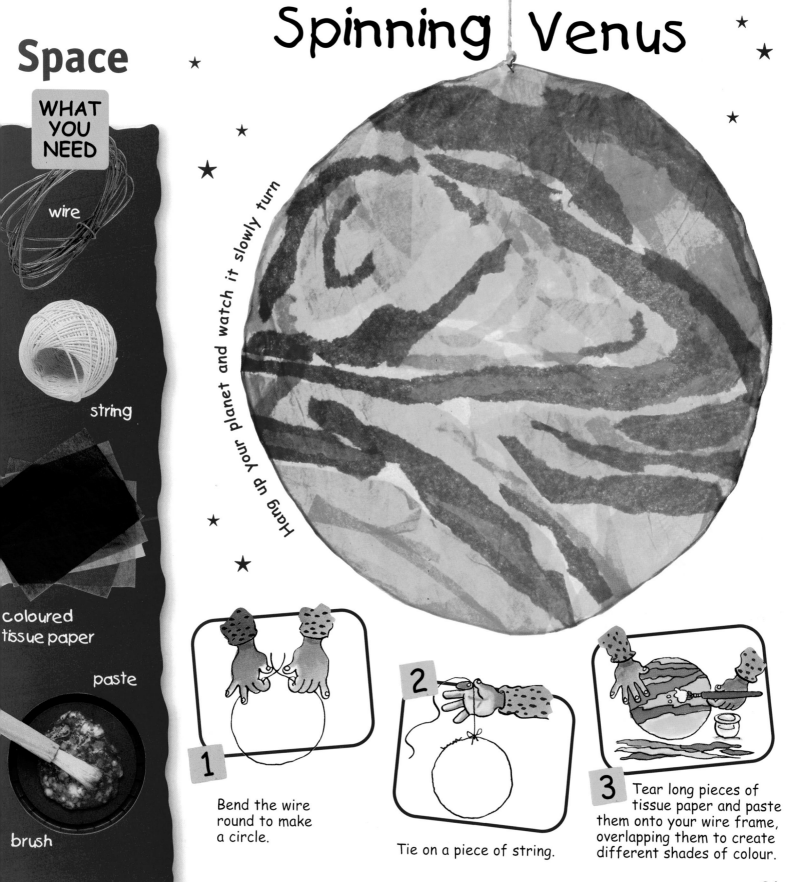

WHAT YOU NEED

wire

string

coloured tissue paper

paste

brush

Hang up your planet and watch it slowly turn

1 Bend the wire round to make a circle.

2 Tie on a piece of string.

3 Tear long pieces of tissue paper and paste them onto your wire frame, overlapping them to create different shades of colour.

31

Rocks in space

NASA

ASTEROID BELT

Most asteroids travel in a region called the Asteroid Belt, which is between 254 million kilometres and 598 million kilometres away from the Sun. They all orbit the Sun in the same direction as the planets, taking between three and six years for each orbit. Ceres is the biggest asteroid and was the first asteroid to be discovered. It was found in 1801. Since then, over 9,000 asteroids have been closely studied, but scientists estimate there are over 50,000 in total.

COLLISION

Scientists think that asteroids were formed billions of years ago from large balls of rock, called protoplanets, each about the size of our Moon. When the protoplanets collided, they broke up into smaller pieces - the asteroids. Most asteroids are thousands of kilometres apart, but they still collide today. If an asteroid is smaller than the one it hits, the collision makes a crater in the larger asteroid. If it is bigger, however, the smaller asteroid may break up and form new, even smaller asteroids.

Circling the Sun between Mars and Jupiter are thousands of rocky objects, called asteroids. These space rocks are also called minor planets because they spin around as they travel, just like planets. Many of the asteroids are no more than a few metres wide, but about a billion measure over one kilometre.

Space

Asteroid belt

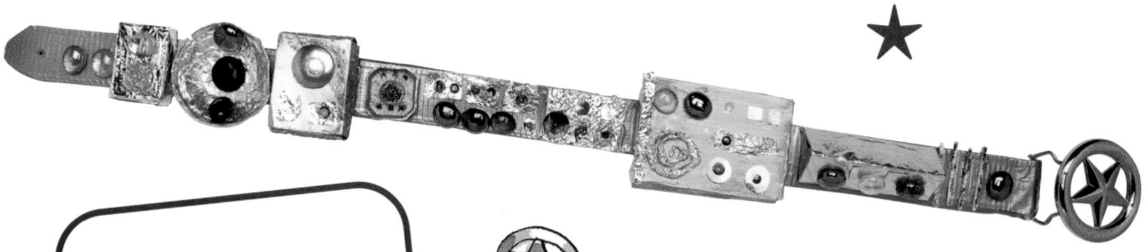

WHAT YOU NEED

- belt
- small cardboard boxes
- silver paint
- glue
- sequins
- foil cases
- glass beads
- paints and brush
- foil
- cocktail sticks

1 Paint an old belt with silver paint.

2 Paint and decorate small boxes with sequins, foil, glass beads and cocktail sticks. Glue these onto the belt.

Dazzle your friends with your funky space belt

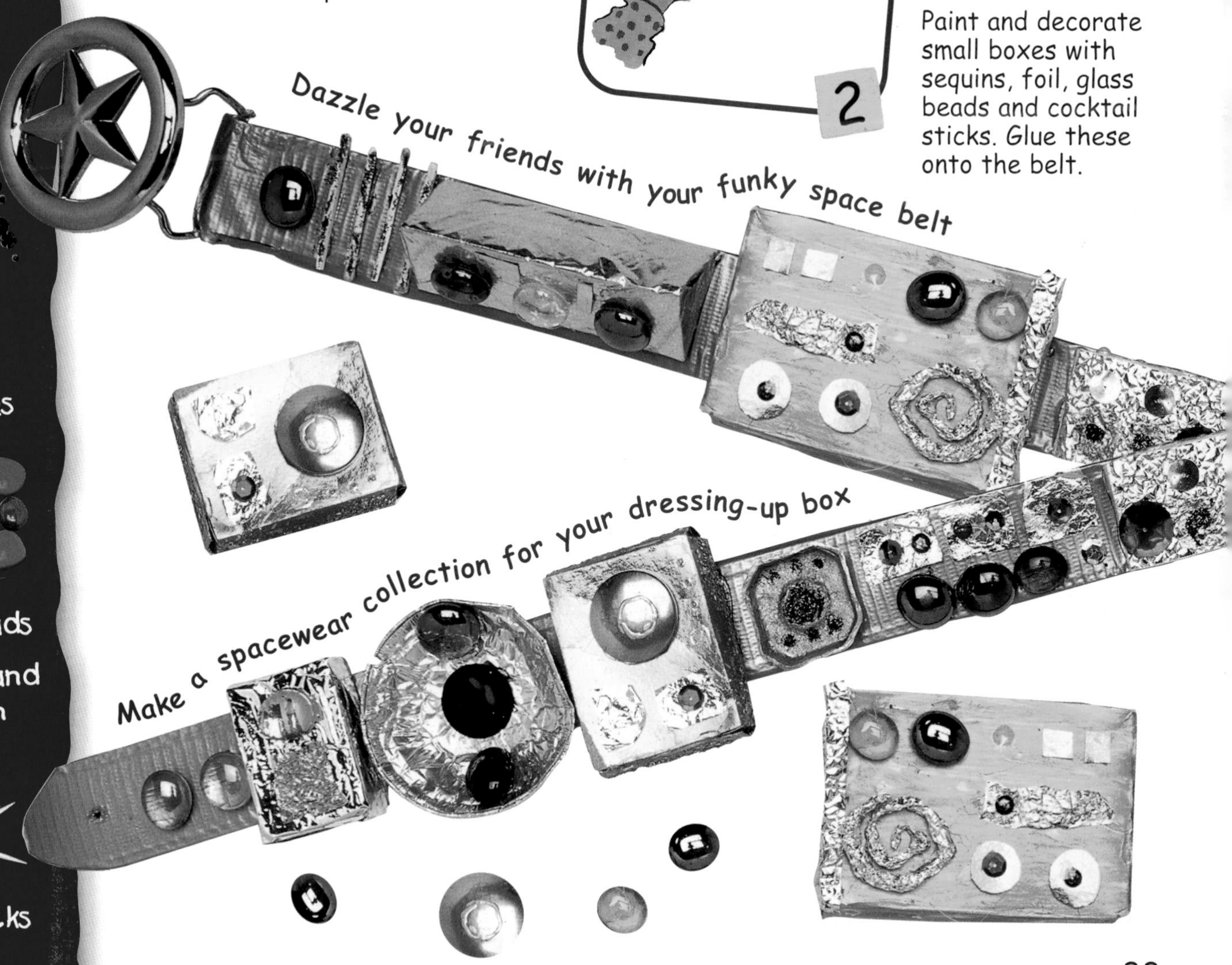

Make a spacewear collection for your dressing-up box

33

Spinning top

Mercury is the closest planet to the Sun, and the second smallest in the solar system after Pluto. It is dry and rocky, its surface cratered by meteorites. Mercury is so close to the Sun you can only see it at certain times of the year. It looks like a bright star and is best seen near the horizon, either in the west just after sunset or in the east just before sunrise.

SWIFT MERCURY

Since it is so close to the Sun, Mercury is the fastest planet to travel around it, travelling at 48 kilometres a second. It takes just 88 days for Mercury to complete one orbit of the Sun compared to Earth's 365 days. It might be quick to orbit the Sun, but Mercury spins slowly on its axis. A day on Mercury lasts the equivalent of 176 days on Earth.

SCORCHED EARTH

The Sun scorches Mercury's surface to incredibly high temperatures. The Sun's rays are seven times stronger on Mercury than they are on Earth, and the planet has so little atmosphere that there is little protection from the heat. Daytime temperatures can soar to over 427°C, while at night they can drop to under –173°C.

CRAGGY PLANET

Mercury's surface is pockmarked with craters, and scarred by ridges and crags. The craters were made by the impact of meteorites that crashed into it billions of years ago. The Caloris Basin is huge and has a central crater more than 1,300 kilometres wide, surrounded by a bull's-eye of several rings of mountains that cover about 3,680 kilometres.

Mercury maze game

WHAT YOU NEED

thick and thin card

pencil

metallic paints

brush

lack paint

glue

★ sequins

marbles

foil

scissors

red paper

1 Draw a large circle onto thick card, cut out and paint a night sky picture on it. Stick on sequins.

2 Cut strips of thin card and cover with silver foil.

3 Stick the strips onto the gameboard from the outside in, leaving gaps for the marbles to pass through, as shown.

4 Cut a circular bull's-eye from red paper. Cut 4 holes big enough to hold the marbles. Glue into the middle of the gameboard.

Send your marbles hurtling through the space maze and get all four to Mercury's bull's-eye!

35

Sky walking

Imagine a place with no air, with temperatures that vary from extreme hot to extreme cold, and where particles of dust travel at such speeds they could kill you. These are just some of the conditions astronauts have to cope with when they travel in space. But the strangest condition is the lack of gravity.

COPING WITHOUT GRAVITY

Gravity is a force that makes objects move towards each other. The Earth's gravity keeps your feet on the ground and makes objects fall down by pulling them towards it. On a spaceship, gravity does not have much effect, and everything floats in the air. It takes a while for an astronaut's body to get used to living in space and many astronauts have 'space sickness' for the first few days or weeks.

STEPS IN SPACE

When astronauts leave the spaceship, they have to wear a space suit which allows them to breathe and protects them from heat, cold and space debris. A backpack linked to the helmet supplies oxygen and takes away carbon dioxide and moisture. The space suit has a radio, so the astronaut can communicate with others inside the spaceship and with ground control back on Earth. The front of the helmet blocks out harmful rays from the Sun. When working on the outside of a space station, a lifeline attaches the suit to the station to stop the astronaut floating away.

Space

WHAT YOU NEED

egg carton

cardboard boxes

glue

wire

paints and brush

foil

sequins

black pen

material

card

black paper

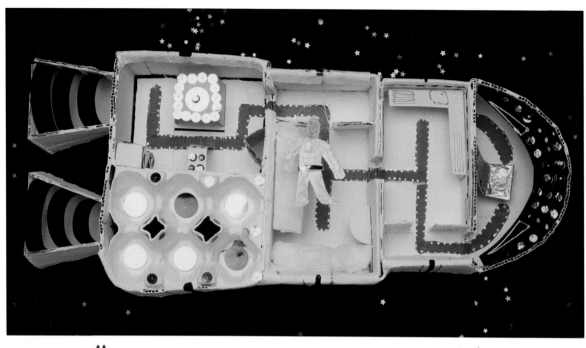

Mount your spaceship against a star-spangled sky

1 Stick a variety of different-sized boxes together to form the shape of a space capsule.

2 Make card turbo rocket engines and glue on strips of black paper, as shown. Glue to capsule. Paint the whole model.

3 Make each compartment different. You could use black paper and sequins to form the bridge in the control room, and glue a commander's foil chair inside.

4 Make beds from fabric and glue into the compartment. Add a bouncy astronaut connected to the bed with wire.

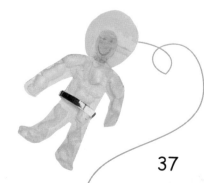

37

Distant planets

Thick, blue clouds cover the planet Neptune

BLUE PLANETS

Uranus and Neptune are known as the blue planets because they are covered in thick, blue clouds. The blue colour comes from methane gas in their atmospheres.

Both Uranus and Neptune are mainly made of water, along with methane and ammonia gases. They both have a number of rings surrounding their equators and a family of moons – Uranus has at least 17 known moons and Neptune has at least eight.

SEASONS AND STORMS

Uranus has eleven rings around its equator, ten of them coal-black and narrow. The unusual thing about Uranus is that it seems to lie on its side as it orbits the Sun. This means it has strange seasons, with each pole cast into total darkness for 42 years, followed by 42 years when the Sun never sets. Neptune has four faint rings of dust. Its atmosphere is struck by violent storms, with winds blowing at about 2,000 kilometres an hour.

ICE DWARF

Pluto is the smallest planet in the solar system, with only one moon. For much of the time, it is the most distant planet from the Sun. Every 248 years, Pluto's orbit takes it closer to the Sun than Neptune, where it stays for about 20 years. When it is nearer the Sun, Pluto's icy surface turns to gas. When it is farther away from the Sun, it becomes completely frozen again.

Far out at the edges of the solar system are the distant giant planets, Uranus and Neptune. They are both about four times the size of Earth. Beyond them, sitting on the very rim of the solar system, is the tiny planet Pluto. Scientists think that Pluto may be one of millions of small, icy worlds that orbit the Sun beyond Neptune, in a region known as the Kuiper Belt.

Space

WHAT YOU NEED

stick

glue

paints and brush

card

pencil

scissors

glitter

Spinning top

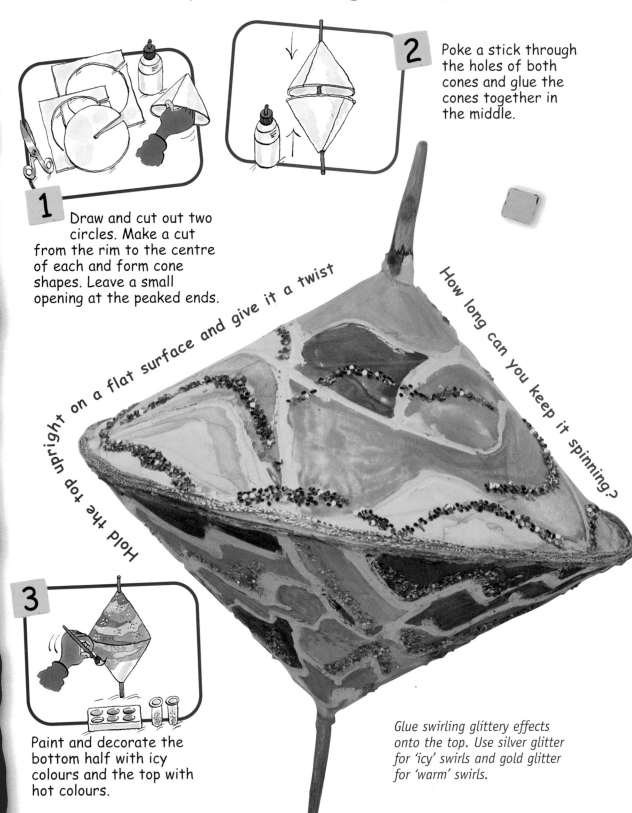

1 Draw and cut out two circles. Make a cut from the rim to the centre of each and form cone shapes. Leave a small opening at the peaked ends.

2 Poke a stick through the holes of both cones and glue the cones together in the middle.

3 Paint and decorate the bottom half with icy colours and the top with hot colours.

Hold the top upright on a flat surface and give it a twist

How long can you keep it spinning?

Glue swirling glittery effects onto the top. Use silver glitter for 'icy' swirls and gold glitter for 'warm' swirls.

39

Trails of light

Every night, bright streaks of light carve across the Earth's skies. These are called meteors, or shooting stars, but they are not stars at all. The streaks are made by fragments of rock and dust as they enter the Earth's atmosphere. As the fragments, called meteoroids, enter the Earth's atmosphere, they cause a lot of friction as they push through the air. This makes them so hot that they burn up, leaving a bright trail of light behind.

COMETS

Comets are giant lumps of snow and dust, like dirty snowballs, which orbit the Sun. When comets travel close to the Sun, the Sun's heat and wind changes their shape. They form a hot, glowing head and two tails. The tails can be more than 100 million kilometres long. Most comets are a long way from the Sun and the planets, at the edge of the solar system, but sometimes they travel closer. This is when we see them in Earth's skies. Certain comets regularly appear in the sky. One such visitor is a beautiful comet called Hale-Bopp. It was last seen in 1997 and will return in about 2007.

CRASH-LANDING

Meteoroids that survive the Earth's atmosphere and reach the ground are called meteorites. About 3,000 meteorites land on the Earth each year. Most are small pieces of rock, but if they are very big, they crash into the ground. The force of impact causes an explosion, blowing a crater out of the ground.

The Hale-Bopp comet streaks across the sky.

Shooting comet

Space

WHAT YOU NEED

wire

sequins

foil

gold thread

bubble wrap

glue

beads

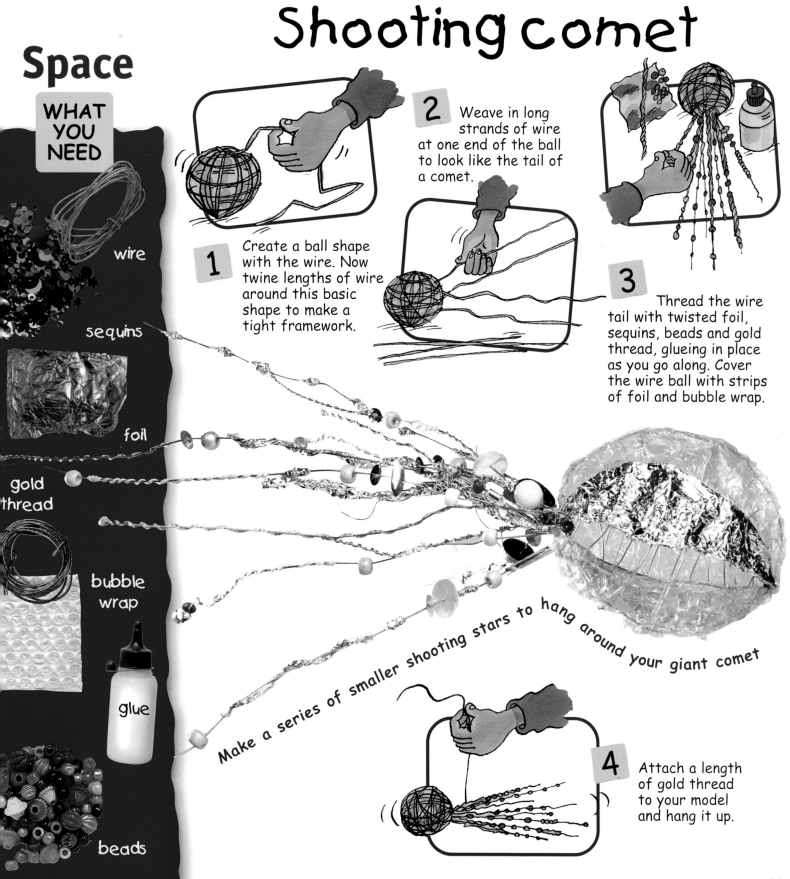

1 Create a ball shape with the wire. Now twine lengths of wire around this basic shape to make a tight framework.

2 Weave in long strands of wire at one end of the ball to look like the tail of a comet.

3 Thread the wire tail with twisted foil, sequins, beads and gold thread, glueing in place as you go along. Cover the wire ball with strips of foil and bubble wrap.

Make a series of smaller shooting stars to hang around your giant comet

4 Attach a length of gold thread to your model and hang it up.

Black holes

Black holes are the most mysterious objects in the Universe. They are invisible monsters that will swallow anything that comes too close, from huge stars to whole families of planets. Even light and time are trapped by their gravity.

DEAD STARS

A black hole is the darkest thing in the Universe. It is a region of space that has such high gravity that nothing can escape from it. A black hole is black because it gives off no light at all – even light cannot travel fast enough to escape its gravity. Black holes are what is left when a giant star explodes and collapses. If the centre, or core, of the star is heavy enough, it is crushed by its own gravity and collapses into a tiny, single point. If anything passes close to the hole, it is dragged inside by the black hole's gravity and disappears from our Universe forever.

PROOF OF EXISTENCE

If a black hole is close to a star, the hole's gravity will pull gas from the star towards it. The gas will spiral around the hole, getting hotter as it is pulled into the hole and giving off X-rays. Scientists can detect these X-rays, and although a black hole itself cannot actually be seen, the X-rays are proof that it exists.

SUPERWEIGHTS

Black holes come in different sizes. Some weigh the equivalent of about 16 Suns, while others are supermassive, weighing billions of times more than the Sun. In 1997, astronomers found evidence of a supermassive black hole at the centre of the Milky Way, and there may be millions more lurking unseen among the stars. Not all black holes are huge: there are some that are no bigger than an atom, although they can still weigh billions of tonnes.

Space

WHAT YOU NEED

large rectangular box with lid

glitter

paint and brush

gold thread

sequins

scissors

gold and silver card

1 Cut the end out of a large rectangular box, leaving the lid intact, and make a small hole at the other end.

2 Paint the box black, inside and out. Decorate the outside with painted stars, sequins and glitter.

3 Paint a white, glittery swirl on the inside of the box around the small hole. Glue a triangular glitter trail on the base, leading towards the far end.

4 Decorate the sides with sequins, splattered paint, and gold and silver card planets.

5 Stick stars on the glitter trail, going from large to small. Cut out and decorate different planets and attach a length of gold thread to each.

Tape the planets to the lid of the box so they hang down

Shine a torch through the hole at the back of your view box to create a shining universe!

Aliens

Do you believe in aliens? Some people think they often visit Earth.

Have you heard about mysterious visitors from outer space who visit Earth in flying saucers? Some people think they are responsible for the strange circles that sometimes appear in our fields. We call these visitors 'aliens', but has anyone ever seen one? Probably not. As far as we know, aliens are just characters in stories or in people's imaginations. But this does not mean they don't exist. Some day, we may well find other life forms in the Universe.

IS THERE ANYBODY OUT THERE?

If aliens exist, it is likely that they are quite different from us. They would only look like us if their planet was identical. All life forms on Earth are based on the chemical element known as carbon. Carbon-based life forms need water in order to develop. So, aliens like us would have to come from a planet where there is carbon and water.

ANOTHER EARTH?

There are millions of stars in the Universe. Some could be similar to our Sun, with planets in orbit around them. Life as we know it on Earth depends on water and oxygen, and can only exist in temperatures that are neither too high nor too low. If a planet was the same distance from its star as we are from our Sun, it might have similar temperatures and be able to support life.

Space

Alien life forms!

WHAT YOU NEED

coloured modelling clay

1

Break off pieces of clay and roll them in your hands to make them soft and easy to model.

2

Form your own alien creatures with funny body shapes...

3

... and roll thin sausage shapes into weird limbs, strange spikes or even alien hairstyles!

4

Now make tiny balls from the clay and use them for bumps, lumps and little green eyes!

Your alien can be whatever you want it to be – after all, who can say you've got it wrong!

You can also create weird alien plants by sticking shaped modelling clay onto wire

Glossary and Index

molten 6

moon 4, 10, 12, 38

Moon 10, 28, 32

nebula (plural: nebulae) A cloud of gas and dust in space. 18

Neptune 4, 38

neutron star The remains of a collapsed star, made from matter compressed so much that it is made entirely from particles called neutrons. 24

nitrogen A gas. 30

North Star (or Pole Star) 14

northern hemisphere 14

nuclear energy Energy that can be released from the particles making up all matter. 8, 24

observatory A place where people use telescopes to study space. 28

orbit The path taken by one object around another in space. 4, 28, 30, 32, 34, 38, 44

oxygen 6, 20, 30, 36, 44

planet 4, 6, 8, 16, 22, 30, 32, 44

photosphere 8

Pleiades 14

Pluto 4, 34, 38

pressure The strength of the force with which something presses. 30

probe 30

prominence 8

protoplanet A large ball of rock, the original content of an asteroid. 32

quasar The very bright core, or centre, of a distant galaxy. 26

radio A radio uses radio waves to send and receive information. 26

radio wave A form of energy that can travel through space and is invisible. 26

reflect 10, 18

Saturn 4, 22

scientist 16, 18, 22, 32, 38, 42

season 6, 38

sky 28, 40

Solar system The Sun and everything that orbits around it. 4, 6, 12, 18, 22, 30 ,38

solar wind 8

southern hemisphere 14

space probe A spacecraft sent to study a planet or space. 30

space station A spacecraft that orbits Earth, on which astronauts live. 20, 36

spaceship/spacecraft 16, 30, 36

star A large ball of gas that gives off light and heat. 8, 14, 18, 24, 26, 30, 34, 42, 44

Sun 4, 6, 8, 10, 22, 30, 32, 34, 36, 38, 42, 44

supergiant star The biggest stars of all, up to 1,000 times bigger than the Sun. 24

supernova (plural: supernovae) A massive star that has exploded, sending out clouds of dust and gas. 24

telescope 12, 14, 18, 22, 26, 28, 30

temperature 8, 34, 44

ultraviolet light An invisible type of light that is given off by very hot objects such as the Sun. 18

Universe 8, 26, 42, 44

Uranus 4, 38

Venus 4, 30

volcano 30

water 6, 16, 20, 30, 38, 44

white dwarf Dwarf stars are the smallest stars. A white dwarf is an old star. 24

X-rays An invisible form of energy similar to light. 26, 42